MAN THE CHURCH OFFICE WITH PURPOSE

God bless you always.

Mary Kokumo
JP
2018

-Memoir of a Worthy Experience

MANAGING THE CHURCH OFFICE WITH PURPOSE

-Memoir of a Worthy Experience

MARY A. KOKUMO

Foreword by Pastor Ghandi Olaoye

INSPIREDSCRIPTS

Managing the Church Office with Purpose - *Memoir of a Worthy Experience*
Copyright © 2018 by Mary A. Kokumo
All rights reserved.

Unless otherwise stated, all scripture quotations are from the King James Version of the Bible.

Published in the USA by Inspired Scripts
www.inspiredscripts.org

ISBN: 978-1984382238

Cover and interior design by Ladak Creative Concepts
www.ladakcreativeconcepts.com

All rights reserved. This book is protected by the copyright laws of the United States of America. This book may not be copied or reprinted for commercial gain or profit. The use of short quotations or occasional page copying for personal or group study is permitted and encouraged with credit to the author. Permission for other uses will be granted upon request. All permission requests should be emailed with Subject: Permissions Coordinator to *marykokumo@yahoo.com*.

Printed in the United States of America

TABLE OF CONTENTS

FOREWORD 7

ACKNOWLEDGEMENTS 9

DEDICATION... 13

INTRODUCTION 15

CHAPTER 1 The Right Foundation 21

CHAPTER 2 Give Honor to Whom Honor is Due 27

CHAPTER 3 Joy Through Service-Getting Stated 35

CHAPTER 4 My Calling and Gifts 41

CHAPTER 5 Prayer, Plan and Prepare............................ 45

CHAPTER 6 Assignment & Tasks Performance 51

CHAPTER 7 Workplace Ethics & Related Skills............ 61

CHAPTER 8 Teamwork Behind the Scene..................... 79

CHAPTER 9 Suggested Samples of Forms Created....... 87

CHAPTER 10 Relationships with All 95

CHAPTER 11 On a Lighter Note-The Funny Side 107

CHAPTER 12 Conclusion.. 111

REFLECTIONS from Pastor Omo Ghandi-Olaoye..... 117

REFLECTIONS from Church Staff and Members....... 129

FOREWORD

Mary A. Kokumo, fondly called "SMK" - has put together a remarkable collection of her experiences working as the Office Manager in one of the toughest organizations to work in ever…Church! Her 18 plus years working at RCCG Jesus House, DC has granted her experience and exposure in many arenas.

In her book "Managing the Church Office with Purpose – Memoir of a Worthy Experience" she shares some of the behind the scenes work she's done over the years as a Church Secretary and Office Manager, and gives many helpful tips and nuggets of information that can be used by any Church Secretary, Office Manager or Administrative Staff in any organization.

This book chronicles how Ms. Kokumo went from working in the corporate world to working in a Faith-based organization. The book can be used as an Office Administrator's manual, with added resources and materials to guide the user along the way.

"Managing the Church Office with Purpose"- Memoir of a Worthy Experience showcases how a single role held in an organization when handled with purpose can yield much experience and exposure with many dividends and rewards.

It demonstrates what happens when a person does their job with intentionality, making them become an invaluable, unforgettable and indispensable asset to their organization.

Ghandi Olaoye
Senior Pastor
THE REDEEMED CHRISTIAN CHURCH OF GOD
JESUS HOUSE, DC

ACKNOWLEDGEMENTS

Many thanks to the Lord God Almighty, who changed my life when I found Jesus and put me on the right path to establish and bless me.

I sincerely thank Pastor Ghandi Olaoye, the Senior Pastor of the Redeemed Christian Church of God – Jesus House, DC. in Silver Spring, Maryland. He is also the RCCG (North America) Regional Pastor (NAR 8) for Special Events and Projects. He has been so instrumental in my life ever since I became a member of the Church. He is truly a man of God. I am forever grateful for his vision, his anointing, his direction and his leadership. Pastor Ghandi has challenged me so much in the area of Restoring Hope & Maximizing Potentials (RHAMP) - always emphasizing that you are not too old to learn and that there are many potentials in you yet untapped. I appreciate you - Pastor Ghandi for agreeing to write the foreword. I say - thank you. I also appreciate to his amiable and supportive wife, Pastor Omo Ghandi-Olaoye for her love towards me.

To the members of staff at Jesus House DC, for your relentless dedication, going above and beyond your duties and providing excellence in all you do; I salute you all. Our teamwork is the best! Sister Mary Kokumo (a.k.a. SMK) finally did it!

My thanks also go to the three Assistant Pastors - Olumide Ogunjuyigbe, Chinyere Olujide and Tunde Ogungbade, and the Church Administrator - Pastor Bimbo Fasosin.

I am grateful to other Ministers, Heads of Department, and JHDC members for their prayers, support and words of encouragement, especially those whose constant prodding applied the necessary pressure to get me serious about this project. I say, thank you!

My appreciation goes to Vivian Anugo –my accountability partner at the Lighthouse Bible-Study Fellowship (Silver Spring 2). She persistently encouraged me. She also spent precious time, proof-reading my manuscript.

I must acknowledge, Toks Akinsanmi for his editing, graphics and art design work and all the creativity invested to get my book printed and published. I say, thank you and may God bless you and make His face shine upon you.

To Ziona Iteoluwakiishi Qing (Sister Z) whose editing skills added value to this effort, I say – thank you. I called on you at the last minute and you rose to the occasion. May God never fail you when you need Him.

To my bosom friends, Pastor Bisi Etuk, Christiana Adeyeri, Felicia Balogun, Clarissa Sarkodee-Adoo, Comfort Akinyele - thank you for your moral support and encouragement – I love you all.

Finally, to my children, Rotimi & Oluyomi

Ogundipe, Seyi & Debbie Omoniyi, the Omoniyi family, the Agbekorode family in the Ogbarukusoro Royal House of Ijebu-Jesha, all grandchildren and relatives back home in Nigeria; I am so grateful for your love and prayers – distance notwithstanding. Thank you for always keeping in touch and wishing me well.

Once again – thank you all!!

"Many thanks to the Lord God Almighty, who changed my life when I found Jesus and put me on the right path to establish and bless me." - SMK

DEDICATION

To the glory of God, this book is dedicated to every staff member (past and present) with whom I have worked at the Jesus House, DC Church Office. My success story today is a product of our teamwork.

Thank you all!

"My success story today is a product of teamwork with all those I have worked with." -SMK

INTRODUCTION

"God is not unjust; he will not forget your work and the love shown him as you have helped his people and continue to help them. We want each of you to show this same diligence to the very end, in order to make your hope sure."
(Hebrews 6:10-11)

After I relocated to the USA from Nigeria in 1997, I found myself dealing with anger and hatred from a broken marriage, business failure and experiences back home that left me fearful. It was hard for me to forgive because I was emotionally, socially and spiritually traumatized. I was in a state of confusion and depression; nothing mattered to me anymore. However, I still held on to the desire to find a Bible-based church, hear the word of God, in the hope that I could be spiritually fulfilled and learn to depend on God.

During my daily Metro train commute to work at the Ghana Embassy, Washington DC., I crossed paths with Mrs. Kehinde Abimbola, who later became a good friend (as I believe God had ordained it). She sensed the pains and challenges that I struggled with and encouraged me to attend services at RCCG- Jesus House, DC.

Some weeks later, I called the church office and Pastor Ghandi picked-up the phone, promising to give me a ride to church on Sunday. True to his word, he came with Pastor Okey Onuzo on Sunday morning to drive me to the Church service. At the end of the service, he arranged for a church member to take me back home. I was really touched by the Pastor's caring attention. Put simply, I started attending church services regularly. Little did I know that God had prepared a place where my life would never remain the same and it was right there in JHDC. It was the perfect opportunity for me to re-dedicate my life to Christ, and the Lord touched me, healed me, and restored me, giving me peace that "passeth all understanding" (Philippians 4: 7).

Through it all, I never completely lost hope because God encouraged me. I continuously prayed and received new life with new hope for the journey ahead. God gave me the spirit of forgiveness for myself first, then my ex-

Introduction

husband, and others who caused me untold pain. I learned how to pray for the strength to move on free of offence. My testimony today is that I can face life with courage to walk and work-out my salvation, no matter what may come my way.

At JHDC, I was received with open arms and found support. I was loved and accepted completely into God's community and family. Mine is a true testimony of how Jesus House, DC is Restoring Hope and Maximizing Potentials (RHAMP). Later in September 1999, I was offered the position of the Church Secretary and was ultimately promoted to Office Manager in Jesus House, DC – the same parish of the Redeemed Christian Church of God (RCCG) that God has used to minister to me, for over 19 years now.

The position of the Church Office Manager in any Faith-based organization is pivotal to church growth and member retention because it is the first port-of-call for current members, visiting pastors, potential members, the community and the public at large. Though challenging, the position requires a tremendous amount of patience, compassion, care, and genuine love. Most of all, it requires effective communication skills with a definite Purpose.

The first thoughts about writing a book on this subject came to me while on vacation in San Francisco, California in November 2006. At that time, I penned some outlines, points and notes but never did anything thereafter. Years later at our annual Leadership Retreat held in Hunt Valley, Maryland, our Senior Pastor Ghandi Olaoye asked everyone a question, "What life ambition would you like to achieve before exiting this world?" I immediately realized that I wanted to write a book, and everyone I shared that Vision with, agreed that it was a great idea.

Procrastination is a very bad habit; so also, is laziness, but God's time is always the best. The Bible states in Ecclesiastes 3 v 11– "He hath made everything beautiful in His time: he will perform and perfect that which He has designed and destined for you".

Finally, when the appointed time came to write this book, the Spirit of God reminded me of all experiences He brought me through. God also raised an overwhelming Body of Witnesses - colleagues, ministers, Lighthouse Silver Spring-2 Bible Study members, family and friends to encourage and support me. Thus, my book was born.

Introduction

I started writing in April 2010 but regrettably abandoned the work in 2014; and did not go back to it until February 2017. The Holy Spirit - my Teacher and Helper, kept reminding me not to let this opportunity to impact lives pass me by. He made me realize how much people needed to be blessed by this book.

Working in God's Vineyard is a privilege and honor that I do not take for granted. It is simply a God-ordained step. I appreciate how far God has brought me – literally out of the miry clay into His marvelous Light. Praise God! I have so much joy serving Him in this capacity. I am spiritually fulfilled, I have prospered and I believe the best is yet to come.

This book is not just a recap of my experiences in the purposeful management of a Church Office; but it is also an effective administrative tool to guide the Administrative team in any church, including the parishes of the Redeemed Christian Church of God and any Faith-based organization.

My prayer is that this book would bless, inspire, motivate and guide all who read it and especially those who follow-through to achieve their desired results. Thank you and God bless.

Mary A. Kokumo

MD - USA

2017

CHAPTER 1

The Right Foundation

> *"According to the grace of God which is given unto me, as a wise master builder, I have laid the foundation, and another buildeth thereon. But let every man take heed how he buildeth thereupon. For other foundation can no man lay than that is laid, which is Jesus Christ." (1 Corinthians 3: 10-11)*

The transition from a former Social Secretary to two former Ambassadors of Nigeria and Ghana to the United States of America in the diplomatic arena, to a Church Office Manager was very challenging and most definitely a learning process for me. The former position entails working and meeting international dignitaries, government officials, top business executives and gurus to establish cordial and bilateral relationships between countries and nationalities (The Foreign Ministry). It is a secular world of civil service and public administration. The latter position in Church, in a religious environment; requires relating to, and serving people with different challenges and spiritual needs. Totally different!

The right foundation was laid by Pastor Ghandi, who was instrumental to making the transition smooth and easy for me. His leadership abilities are so unique that it produces good organization and facilitates growth. God has gifted every human being with different talents with which to edify others and glorify God.

First of all, I found Jesus House, DC to be the place where God rebuilt me and my faith, so that I could grow. It is the right place where God helped me to recognize my God-given talents and granted me the strength to pursue all my God-given goals. It is a place where the spirit of excellence is channeled purposefully, hope is restored and potentials are maximized. It is important for me to recognize that God feeds me and strengthens me to serve His people because I cannot give what I don't have.

My position has given me the opportunity to meet with great men and women of God like Daddy & Mommy Adeboye, the General Overseer of the Redeemed Christian Church of God – RCCG worldwide and his wonderful wife. In this position, I have also met Pastor & Dr. James Fadel, Dr. Myles Munroe (of blessed memory), Dr. Mensa Otabil, Pastor Agu Irukwu, Dr. A.R. Bernard, Les Brown, Dr. Paula White, Dr. Ayo Oritsejafor, Rev. George Adegboye, Bishop Alfred Owens, Pastor James Bamidele

Sturdivant, Pastor Eskor Mfon (of blessed memory), Rev. Funmi Adetuberu, Pastor Peter Amenkhianen, Pastor Femi Atoyebi, Pastor Tony Rapu, Minister Michelle McKinney-Hammond, Rev. Jackie McCullough, Prophetess Francina Norman, Pastor Sola Olowokere, Pastor Ropo Tusin, Pastor Bayo Adewole, Pastor Leke Sanusi, Pastor Tola Odutola, Pastor Wale Akinsiku, Evangelist Oguazi Onyemobi, Pastor Matel Okoh, Apostle Daniel Wilson, Pastor Bayo Adeyokunnu, Pastor Sola Oludoyi, Bishop George Bloomer, Pastor Chris Adetoro, Pastor Bayo Fadugba and some RCCG Pastors God is using in the tri-state area or DMV.

I have also had the privilege of meeting many Business, and Government dignitaries from within and outside America; including great Professionals and Achievers from Nigeria – who passed through JHDC as invited guest ministers at many regular, special, annual events and programs. Gospel artistes Mary-Mary, Vickie Winans, Tye Tribbett, Tim Godfrey, Eben, Kunle Meshida, Solomon Lange, etc. and our in-house gospel artists like JHDC Mass Choir, Dara Adewole, Jumbo Ane, PCE Crew, Ope Boroffice and others form an elite group of Music Ministers that I have had the privilege to meet in person. I cannot forget our gospel MCs who have moderated many events with sanctified humor like Toye Gansallo, Jedi Ayoola, Wamilele, Busola Grillo, Godwin Eremah, Olumide Ayoola and others. They have contributed to the powerful ministrations that have powerfully impacted my life greatly. I will like to appreciate Vomoz Media and The Kingdom TV for their efforts and relentless support in spreading the gospel using their platform.

My position has brought me respect and love from all and sundry by the grace of God, with blessings I could not have imagined possible. The immense knowledge gained from this position cannot be over-emphasized. I have enjoyed powerful ministrations, leadership trainings, empowering meetings and miraculous retreats, conferences and conventions, workshops and seminars. These experiences helped me develop ever-increasing leadership qualities that daily help me to function creditably as I serve God's people.

Everyone possesses leadership potentials – you just need to find the right avenues that would expose them and bring them to fruition. Also, you need to find an avenue to bring it out from within. I remember one such opportunity, when I gave a presentation on Church Office Administration, particularly as it pertains to the office of a Church Secretary at a Workers Meeting some years ago. It was received with great enthusiasm. That seed was sown and was ultimately nurtured in intense

> *Everyone possesses leadership potentials – you just need to find the right avenues that would expose them and bring them to fruition.*

prayers for God to reveal His own will through this book assignment. This book project brought about purpose that would align with God's plan for my life. This began the idea of intense prayer for God to reveal His direction to pursue this goal and make it an assignment with a purpose that aligns with God's plan for my life.

"Everyone possesses leadership potential – one needs to find an avenue to bring it out from within." -SMK

CHAPTER 2

Give Honor to whom Honor is Due

> *"Honor them that have the rule over you, and submit yourselves: for they watch for your souls, as they that must give account, that they may do it with joy, and not with grief: for that is unprofitable for you." (Hebrew 13:17)*

Pastor Ghandi-Olaoye

I heard about Jesus House, DC through a good friend - Mrs. Kehinde Abimbola, who later invited me to church. She gave me the church office phone number and encouraged me to call. A month after her invitation, I called and Pastor Ghandi picked-up the phone. I did not have a car at the time, and therefore had no means of getting to church, especially on a cold North-Eastern day. There was also no Sunday bus service along the Forest Glen area of Silver Spring at the time. He promised to pick me up. And true to his word, Pastor Ghandi showed-up at my door at 8.30am prompt, on Sunday with Dr. Okey Onuzo, a visiting guest minister. He gave me a ride to church and at the end of the service, found a member to drive me back home. This gesture was so caring that the memory of it remains with me till this day.

I became a member of JHDC from June 1999. In August of 1999, Pastor Ghandi saw me in Church and asked me to meet with him in his office after service but I didn't on that day. He saw me again two weeks later and asked to meet after service. Finally, I obliged and the meeting seemed less of a meeting and more of an interview. At the end of the meeting, he offered me the position of the Church Secretary. My first impression of him was that he was frank. His last question before I left his office was: "I can be very tough so do you think you can work with me?" My answer was "God-willing and with patience I will perform well."

This position was ordained by God because it was just at the time when I was contemplating changing my job to another Embassy in Washington DC. In September 1999, I resumed at the Church Office, where I met Toyin Fabayo (now Mrs. Bakare), Udachi Otumba (now Mrs. Uzobuihe), Yinka Agunbiade, and Folami Odusanya – in all we were six (6) members of staff. Deacon Valentine Nwandu was the Church Administrator and Accountant at that time.

Relationships

Destiny is divine but the fulfillment involves yielded individuals. Pastor Ghandi is truly a servant/man of God and my spiritual father. I am a woman under his authority both spiritually and officially. He has been an instrument of God in my life - encouraging and supporting me positively, even challenging me to do more. I know he wants the best for me. Excellence is central to serving under his leadership.

My Boss

I see Pastor Ghandi as a boss who protects the reputation of JHDC by all means possible; promoting high performance levels in church operations so the Church could be a one-of-a-kind church that other churches can emulate and learn from. He is very neat and extremely organized. He dislikes dirty and filthy surroundings.

Leadership Character

Pastor Ghandi's leadership character traits standout in his relationships with people. He is very respectful, humble and he deals with everyone with integrity. He has a big heart and he is also very generous. He's written me checks as gifts on many birthdays. He returns from annual vacations with gifts for staff members including me. Over the years, Pastor Ghandi has rewarded my diligence and hard-work with multiple promotions, salary increases and bonuses.

Influence

As my spiritual father, Pastor Ghandi has influenced and impacted my life through his teachings and sermons over the years. Typing-up all his sermon notes is not only an honor; but it has also proven to be an amazing blessing because God has used his sermon notes to personally minister to me as a Believer while typing them up. These sermon notes are treasures; I am blessed to be part of documenting it for posterity. I also believe that I have influenced and impacted him positively with my faithfulness, trust-worthiness, honesty and hard-work. He's always encouraging and giving me positive feedback, urging me to do more.

I will never forget one particular way he has blessed me. He granted the approval for the Church to sponsor the adjustment of my immigration status as an employee in 2005. The filing process and payment began in earnest with an Attorney. To the glory of God, it was approved and I received my Green Card. By the Grace of God, I am a US Citizen now. Pastor Ghandi was very happy for me, and I am forever grateful to him.

My Prayer

When I go down memory lane, remembering many details about my association with Pastor Ghandi as my Senior Pastor and boss, I am just so grateful to God. So, my prayer is that the Lord God will continue to increase his anointing. The Lord will bless him and his family abundantly. He will prosper in everything that he lays his hand to do; and it shall be well with him and his family in Jesus Name.

(THE SENIOR PASTORS – GHANDI & OMO OLAOYE)

Pastor Omo Ghandi-Olaoye

My relationship with Pastor Omo has been very close with mutual respect and admiration. Over the years, I find her to be very articulate, detail-oriented, meticulous, and administratively thorough. She can be very strict at times when she wants certain task to be performed well. She is my motivator and encourager who inspires me to achieve more in life. As a Minister of God, she is a powerful preacher – very eloquent in the delivery of her sermons. Her ministrations always impact me positively. She is a prayer warrior who strongly believes in the efficacy of Prayer. Her life testifies to miracles from the God who answers the effectual, fervent prayer of the righteous (James 5: 16).

As a Church First Lady, I am impressed by her poise and confidence. She commands respect and I see her as a worthy example to the body of Christ in her leadership role, empowering women and restoring hope to all. As a devoted Pastor's wife, she is a virtuous woman. As a Mother, she's loving and caring to everyone who comes in contact with her. She is very jovial and has a good sense of humor.

I had the honor of driving her to/from her antenatal appointments during her pregnancy; for which she was always grateful. After the delivery of her twin girls - Fehintolu and Toluni, I gladly joined the team of caregivers whenever she needed me. It's been a great privileged to assist her at home and at her children's school from time to time. The twins are very comfortable having me around. They have grown into beautiful young ladies, sometimes shy but with good manners and godly character.

I can attest to how generous Pastor Omo is because she has blessed me with many gifts over the years. The church office staff members also appreciate the cakes, chocolates, meat-pies, sausage rolls, cookies, jollof rice and all the different assortments of food she sends our way.

An example of her generosity was when I informed her of my plans to celebrate my sixtieth (60th) birthday. She took it upon herself to set-up a special committee to plan and organize the celebration. She was there personally to support me morally, spiritually and financially to make sure it was a joyous and successful celebration. She has always been a blessing in my life.

My prayer is that she will never be found wanting in her service to the Lord God Almighty. May God reward her labor of love. The peace and joy of the Lord will be with her; and her children shall be successful in life in Jesus Name.

CHAPTER 3

Joy through Service-Getting Started

> *"In everything that he undertook in the service of God's temple and in obedience to the law and the commands, he sought his God and worked wholeheartedly. And so he prospered." (2 Chronicles 31:21)*

The importance of experienced human resources cannot be over-emphasized in successful Church operations. For a fast-growing church like Jesus House DC, there are professional and well-experienced people in roles such as Accounting & Finance, Counseling, Administration, Community Outreach, Ministry Operations, Member Services, Property management, Information Technology, Web Design and state of the art Technology to mention just a few.

The position of Church Secretary & Office Administrator requires a College degree and Computer proficiency in Microsoft Office Suite: Word, Excel, Power Point and Publishing etc. Other useful skills include interpersonal skills, communication skills, strong organizational/administrative skills, and leadership skills. In addition, it is important to be able to multi-task and be a reliable team-player. Since we live in the Internet age, being able to navigate the internet to promote productivity is essential. Therefore hardware, software, indeed all systems must be in place and functioning optimally. Elexio Database, Power Church, Purpose Driven, Church Management Systems, and Servant Keeper come highly recommended in my experience of software useful for Church Database management.

Currently, JHDC uses Elexio Database to manage membership, activities, involvement, attendance, groups' mail merge, reports, mailing, email administration and much more. Most of the technologies recommended here integrate with cloud a technology that not only manages online giving and donations; but also facilitate telework. These technologies have built-in appointments and reminders to make sure important dates and meetings are not forgotten.

Smooth church office operations need five (5) components:

The Office Layout, Work Area, Records Management, Health & Safety; Fire and Rescue Considerations.

a. The Office Layout:

It is important to provide enclosed office spaces, shared rooms, open spaces in cubicle format easy access to desktop computers etc.

b. Work Area

Standard equipment includes basic office furniture, and cabinet for office supplies, printers, phones, fax, writing, etc. Printer and copiers for heavy network use, are best located in a separate space.

Mass-mailing flyers etc. to members is cost-saving and a frequent operation. Therefore, it's important to create a mailing Space for handling bulk mail dispatch or daily incoming mails.

c. Records Management Space

Simple alphabetical system filing and retrieval of documents is the best approach. Cabinets with active files to which you have regular access should be kept in your office. Closed and old files with important documents can be stored in boxes. The importance of retaining documents in safe or secure boxes cannot be overstated. Filing and Office supplies include filing cabinets: steel or wood, folders, labels, index cards, and general office supplies must be in adequate supply.

d. Health & Safety Consideration

Proper building and safety code must be adhered to. All Health and Safety inspections must be completed in compliance with the Law as well as local county guidelines.

Church building access must be restricted to meetings and services and other related programs. A Security alarm system is important for theft and break-in deterrence and reduction. Attention should be given to potential hazards such as snow removal in driveways, sanding or salting icy side-walks, and parking lots lighting.

e. First Aid Kit/Box

Every staff member must know where the First Aid kit is located, for prompt emergency response before calling 911 or the Police. Standard kits usually contain medical essentials including but not limited to:

- Pain medication e.g. Ibuprofen, Aspirin, Motrin, Aleve, Advil

- Adhesive Bandages of different sizes, Antibiotic cream or ointment to prevent infections

- Gauze, Cotton Wool, Antiseptic Cleansing Wipes, Assorted bandages

- Antacid and more.

e. Fire Alarm Safety & Rescue Considerations

Fire Drills can be scheduled with the Fire Marshals in the Division of Fire Prevention and Code Compliance. Church staff members only or the entire congregation would be drill participants as necessary. Annual Fire Alarm Safety and Rescue inspection of sundry equipment is absolutely important. This includes the Fire Alarm System, Sprinklers, Mechanical & Pump valves and Elevators to make sure that all areas within the building are up to code and pose no threat to lives and property. Elevators and other service equipment must be serviced, repaired with date-tags showing due dates for re-certification and inspection by the Fire Marshal visible.

The Utility rooms such as electrical, mechanical, plumbing, security alarm system, communication system, stairways and all exits-entrances must not be used as storage. All these areas must be free of combustible materials, and allow for the easy flow of member traffic should there be any fire incident. All emergency lights, smoke detectors, exit sign lights and pull stations must function well and remain in service. Fire Department Connection (FDC) signage and other signs must be installed and posted on designated doors to indicate locations visible to Fire Fighters and approaching Fire apparatus.

CHAPTER 4

My Calling and Gifts

> *"Having then gifts differing according to the grace that is given to us." (Romans 12: 6)*
>
> *"And he gave some, apostles; and some, prophets; and some, evangelists; and some, pastors and teachers. For the perfecting of the saints, for the work of the ministry, for edifying of the body of Christ." (Ephesians 4:11-12)*

God provides spiritual gifts or talents to His people for use in serving Him. I believe all Christians have all of the gifts mentioned in the Bible, in varying degrees. My ability to anticipate the needs of members and to joyfully assist them has enabled me to serve successfully. As I mature in my Christian life and walk with God, the Grace and the knowledge of God through the study of His word has produced much spiritual growth and transformation of my faith.

It has always been my vision to become an excellent and seasoned manager using my God-given potentials in the performance of duties supporting the Vision in Jesus House, DC – which is: Restoring Hope and Maximizing Potentials (RHAMP). God enlightened my eyes to see the desired end-result, which in turn motivates and empowers me to purposefully work towards my goal.

> *I am also open to cultural changes, creativity and innovation.*

Developing as a Believer and a World Citizen, involves continuous learning. In my experience, being open to learning constantly has equipped me and facilitated my constant growth and being increasingly better at what I do. I am also open to cultural changes, creativity and innovation. These are important agents that have helped me to improve what I do; and have inspired me to come-up with new ideas or new way of functioning in my position for higher job performance and fulfillment.

Without a doubt, I am a purpose-driven administrator because my focus is always on achieving the desired results to God's glory and for the blessing of His

People. This purpose has ignited my passion to be committed to high-level performance in what I do daily, and doing this daily strengthens me to even strive for more excellence in every area of life. My fundamental mission therefore, is to responsibly coordinate the daily administration of the Church Office in the most efficient and effective way possible.

The roles and responsibilities I have been assigned include the following: -

- Coordinate and supervise the administrative functions of the church; formulating and implementing appropriate administrative strategies and processes for the efficient operations of the church office.

- Manage the Church front office and ensure that it operates optimally and is adequately maintained.

- Provide vendor management and coordination, sourcing and ordering of office supplies and monitoring to ensure vendors, subcontractors, and service providers are in compliance with all legal guidelines and procedures under the building code.

- Maintain the Church calendar and disseminate ministerial and departmental information on events and activities to Church members by email, SMS text message, phone tree messages, written correspondences and through the JHDC website at: www.jesushousedc.org.

- Maintain and manage the use of the Petty Cash.

- Ensure accuracy and timeliness in support functions preparatory to all JHDC church programs and activities.

- Coordinate and oversee logistics and procurement activities and/or functions.

- Prepare various analyses and reports required by the Office of the Pastor about general administration and activities.

- Maintain JHDC's fixed assets/inventory and generate reports as and when needed.

- Perform any other duties as directed.

Evidently, the scope of my responsibilities includes working closely with the Office of the Senior Pastor, Church Administrator, Ministry Operations, Member Services/Project Management Office, Accounting, and all Ministries and Departments. My role and responsibilities ensure that the JHDC Church Office runs seamlessly.

CHAPTER 5

Pray, Plan and Prepare

"And all things, whatsoever ye shall ask in prayer, believing, ye shall receive." (Matthew 21:22)

Commit thy works unto the Lord, and thy thoughts (plan) shall be established. (Proverbs 16:3)

The lyrics of a popular lyrics of a popular Old-School Gospel Chorus goes like this:

"Prayer is the Key, Prayer is the key,

Prayer is the master key,

Jesus started with prayer and ended with prayer,

Prayer is the master key."

Prayer is a vital communication channel between me and my Maker – The Almighty God. I will strongly advise that you develop a lifestyle of Prayer – on your own and with others. Weekly prayer meetings and fellowship at your workplace holds the key to setting-up the church office atmosphere for success – yours and others. Do not discount the importance of daily prayers in your personal life and your office. God requires His children to stay in constant connection with Him and this we must do through Praying without ceasing.

Prayer empowers, prayer gives clarity and daily direction for the tasks ahead. Ultimately, it is the core of my ability to fulfill my purpose. It improves your spirituality in a secular world, and I have personally found that it makes me a happy worker. On a daily basis, I would advise that you do the first things first. Put God First. Fill your Spirit-man daily through prayers based on the Word of God. Jesus is our example, and He prayed every time especially before doing anything. So, make Jesus your firm foundation. Start by thanking God as you begin your work-day. Appreciate Him for the opportunity of allowing you to serve in His vineyard. Daily reading of the Word is essential to your spiritual growth because the Word of God enlightens and illuminates the mind. Let the compassion, care and love of Christ flow through your heart as you perform your tasks. You cannot give what you do not have. Let God give you what you need to pass on to His people. The more you LIVE in the WORD,

> *Let the compassion, care and love of Christ flow through your heart as you perform your tasks.*

the more you are able to exercise the Fruit of the Spirit which is "love, joy, peace, longsuffering, kindness, goodness, faithfulness, gentleness, self-control" (Galatians 5: 22-23).

Through my working experience, I have come to understand and accept how to be inclusive towards members of different cultures, diverse backgrounds and lifestyles. This is simply the way to eliminate the spirit of discrimination. Church is a "come as you are" place – like a hospital with people coming-in with different challenges and situations. It also helps for you to make positive confessions throughout the day, to remind you to render excellent, effective and efficient service to one and all. Always do more than is required of you, and do it well.

Your goal or objective is to perform administrative duties and functions in a manner that will glorify and honor God. Invariably, God is your ultimate Boss.

Understanding this would make a positive impact on how you serve in any position you find yourself in life. Showing you care, builds trust and confidence within the community of church members. Remember that your actions and attitudes to work will determine your success; which can increase your blessings in every sphere of your life and take you to the next level. You must be comfortable with people to develop relationships. A simple smile goes a long way. Be pleasant. Ask about their family, and you will be surprised that members will start to talk and open-up to you. Love everyone unconditionally and maintain the highest level of care and concern for others.

Understanding the importance of good Customer Service also means giving undivided attention, treating people well, and providing useful information in a timely manner to members, ministers, departments and the public as requested or required.

What is the Customer Service Approach?

1. It is the willingness to serve others in an excellent manner.

2. It is an organization's ability to serve customers' wants and needs.

3.   It is the ability to provide a service or product in a way that it has been promised.

In the Faith-based context, it is essential that you are polite and friendly because your interactions with members, ministers and non-members, indeed everyone who comes through your office daily; still falls within the scope of customer service relations. My ability to fully apply customer service ethics has been the bedrock of the good relationships I have church-wide. God has enabled me to leverage this into solid trust and confidence with members; who feel free to always come back to me, believing that I will assist them with the necessary information. Doing this sends the message to members that you are in control and can handle requests without gossiping about it.

Often times I am the point of contact for every announcement and/or information that needs to be transmitted by email or sometimes through the JHDC in-house TV media outreach initially called 'Good News Network' now Rhamp TV. Therefore, I am always at the center of every piece of information including upcoming events and programs.

In dealing with members and people in general, you must choose your words carefully, be very patient and an active listener so you can understand more. You must pay attention and stay focused. Whether you realize it or not, your actions and attitude to work can determine not only your performance and success, but that of others too.

Remember to make Jesus your firm foundation. With Jesus, all things are possible including your being able to perform with excellence. Live with the consciousness that God is watching you. Always go above and beyond the call of duty on any assignment and do it well. Be compassionate with church members and they will feel comfortable with you.

I consider my work in the Lord's vineyard a sacred privilege and I appreciate the honor given me. I do not take it for granted that the Lord ordered my steps into this path.

CHAPTER 6

Assignments and Task Performance

"Jesus saith unto them, My meat is to do the will of him that sent me and to finish his work (task.)" John 4:34

According to lessons learned from a recent Management 101 course on Planning, Organizing, Staffing, Controlling, and Leading, there are basic functions necessary to achieve set goals for managing any office. To delegate, set deadlines and priorities, achieve team work, get feedback and give rewards, there is a need to motivate and encourage employees' performance and productivity.

Stephen R. Covey – who authored "7 Habits of Highly Effective People", emphasized the use of Time Management:

• Begin with the end in mind – envision the big picture or results ahead.

Managing the Church Office With Purpose

- Think Win-Win – that it can be done and done well.

- Be Proactive – to anticipate growth, development, change and adapt to it.

- Sharpen your skills – in communication and leadership through training.

- Put first things first – prioritize, have a To-do list, creatively use block plans in calendars.

- Avoid procrastination – respond immediately, don't delay till tomorrow what can be done today.

Synergize – make it a habit of doing things together to achieve better results.

- Synergize – make it a habit of doing things together to achieve better results.

The operating procedures for my position are as follows:

Duties are done (Daily/Weekly/Monthly):

1. Front Office: With polite, friendly and customer-oriented service - attend to members and visitors/guests promptly. Provide information needed by phone/email/fax/text and written correspondences courteously and promptly.

Assignments and Task Performance

2. Telephone Calls: Pick up phone calls at the 3rd Ring to answer: "IDENTIFY THE NAME OF ORGANIZATION, YOUR NAME AND ASK – "HOW CAN I HELP YOU". Know the list of extension numbers provided for easy transfer of calls. Answer with a soft and pleasant tone of voice at all times.

3. Voice Mail: Listen to voice messages, return or follow up on calls promptly and delete messages where necessary.

4. Emails: Check the Microsoft Outlook Emails regularly and reply/forward enquiries and other information within 24/48 Hours. Delete junk/unsolicited emails.

5. Mails & Packages: Pick up and receive daily mails from the Mailbox and receive packages from FedEx/UPS/DHL/USPS Courier Services with a smile that is carried in your voice. Sort and deliver mails and packages appropriately to the right office in a timely manner.

6. New Guest Reception Cards: Using Elexio Database, enter basic data information of members and guests from the reception card – mark as checked when

done, so the system can generate letters of Appreciation. Print out such letters and attach address labels - insert postage stamps using the Postage Meter Mail Station and drop for mailing at the nearest Post Office or for pickup by the Mailman.

7. This Week @ (Insert the name of the Church): You may create this weekly event and send out by email to all members every Monday. Manage and follow the Events Calendar to guide you on programs for the week. Proof-read, edit, and post on the church website and email to members on the email list.

8. Baby-Naming Ceremony: Check for emails from the Joyful Mothers Ministry or calls from individual members who recently delivered babies. Register & enter necessary information first in Monthly Planner – update and send information by email attachment to the Associate Pastor.

9. Reminder Announcements for Sunday & Holy Communion Services: Use Microsoft Word to update changes of appropriate Date and weekly upcoming programs & events. Update and announce new births (as necessary).

Assignments and Task Performance

10. Prayer Requests: for Congregational Prayers on Sunday Service – check and pickup prayer requests from the Prayer Request Box at the Foyer Area every Friday. Some may be sent by email. Collate requests from all sources, edit and print. Update Prayer Requests and print for pickup on Sunday by the Protocol Department.

11. Child/Baby Dedication: at JHDC, this is done during the 3rd Sunday Service every month. Individual members will call or complete request forms. Record and register necessary information of the baby's (Name/DOB/Hospital/Sex) in Monthly Planner. Collate names and prepare Baby Dedication Certificates and letters to each family registered, get it signed by the Pastor. Do address labels for envelopes; insert signed Certificates/Letters for presentation by the Associate Pastor on the 3rd Sunday.

12. Service of Songs: check the calendar of events to select a Saturday date @ 6pm and advise the bereaved member or family. Provide Technical and Choir support forms to be completed and given to their HODs. Provide a sample program of service that can be updated with their information.

13. Send email reminders to the Associate Pastor – cc: other Assistant Pastors as well. Meanwhile email

ministers/workers for their information and encourage support for the service.

14. JHDC Marriages/Certificates: The Senior Pastor and the Minister in charge for Marriage Ministry must have awareness of the status of the relationship. Advice couples to see both Pastors in person. Check the calendar of events to select a date or if date is selected, check calendar if date is available (and does not clash with other events). Provide pre-marriage counseling form for completion and registration. Provide Technical, Video Wall Screen and Choir support forms to be completed and given to the respective HODs. Provide a sample program of service that can be updated with their information. Get a copy of the formal invitation and prepare draft of Marriage Certificate for Calligraphy Studio Artwork. Send reminder by email to the Associate Pastor – cc: Assistant Pastors as well. Follow up till the date of wedding ceremony.

15. JHDC Online Store Orders by Email – If for Audio Tape - forward to HOD (Audio Tape Ministry) to process order. Audio Tape would be subsequently provided for mailing. For Video Tape - forward to HOD (Video Tape) to process order. Video Tape would be subsequently provided for mailing. Create and prepare JHDC packing slip and mail with a copy of the order form, while keeping a copy in file.

Assignments and Task Performance

16. JHDC Monthly Spiritual & Progress Report: this is a collation of monthly attendances, sermons preached, spiritual activity and other related reports that are emailed to the RCCG (North America) Central Office.

17. Pickup monthly attendance sheets from the Ushering Department to include counts by the Protocol Department. These figures will include the numbers for Men, Women (Adults) COP/JGEN & Caleb Crew Teenage ministries for 1st/2nd/3rd services on Sunday & Wednesday (Holy Communion/Lighthouse Fellowships) attendance counts. Compare both figures and take the highest. Pick up the list of sermon titles from the Audio Tape Ministry for such service days. Email to RCCG (North America) Central Office – cc: Office of the General Overseer.

18. Monthly Birthday Cards: Using Elexio Database, go to Report, click Custom Search and look/click on JHDC Members Birthdays- User Selected. On Report option click Labels. On Report Filters, delete old month. On Field click: Birthday Month. On Operator click: is exactly. On Values click: Select Month. Click: Add search criteria and click: Run Report. Finally insert address labels, print and stamp the Senior Pastor's signature and best wishes on Birthday Cards, stuff into envelopes, seal, attach address labels and add postage stamps ready for mailing. An Electronic

Birthday Greetings is emailed every month to members as well.

19.   OTHERS

• Liaise with Montgomery County-MD Offices and the Montgomery Police Department to obtain licenses/permits for Special Events. Submit the application with the Certificate of Liability Insurance two months before the event. A similar Certificate of Liability Insurance is required with the application when the Church wants to use public facilities/buildings for church events. The same procedure needs to be followed for the use of Recreational Park for Mini-Olympic/Picnic, Civic Centers, and other State or County properties. A yearly license renewal is required for the Basement Kitchen and Olive Tree Café.

• Supervise and track inventory/provision of office supply and the supply of drinks, water, and food orders for ministerial use via vendors such as Office Depot, Staples, Costco, and Caterer Services. Purchase Orders must be approved for supply to be purchased and catered for.

20.   Facility/Logistics & Janitorial

• Coordinate janitorial functions plus Repairs, Replacement including routine inspections etc.

Assignments and Task Performance

- Check and maintain the general cleanliness and rearrangement. Also, check that vendors/service providers to do their jobs right and comply with church standards/guidelines. Materials can be purchased from the Home Depot upon approval of Purchase Order.

- Coordinate the maintenance of JHDC fleet of vehicles which includes Motor Vehicle registration/renewals, auto insurance, emission inspections to car wash/detailing and vehicle repairs.

- Coordinate and ensure that JHDC and its premises comply with the Health & Safety and Security inspections set by Montgomery County.

- All Security Alarms and Lock-up must be done and strictly adhered to, according to the routine service and schedule roster.

- The Elevator is serviced regularly to pass MD Inspection and license renewals annually.

- Fire Drills to be scheduled by the Church Administrator for church members and staff awareness as needed.

"According to lessons learned from a recent Management 101 course on Planning, Organizing, Staffing, Controlling, and Leading, there are basic functions necessary to achieve set goals for managing any office." -SMK

CHAPTER 7

Workplace Ethics & Related Skills

"Be ye strong therefore, and let not your hands be weak: for your work shall be rewarded." (2 Chronicles 15:7)

Communication

Throughout my years as Office Administrator, the Lord has given me peculiar skills which He has enabled me to develop even further. I am a woman of few words, not because I don't have anything to say, but because unnecessary conversations take too much effort. I communicate much more in writing and therefore I express myself better that way.

A simple definition of Communication is the need to express yourself clearly, to be understood in the expression and exchange of ideas. It is a two-way process between the sender and receiver through a medium. Therefore, the ability to communicate very well is a highly-desirable skill. Through communication you can be loving, welcoming, spread or share the Word, are relatable and give attention to members and hopefully connect with others to share the love of God. We need to develop this ability to effectively communicate and become the leaders that God has called every one of us to be.

An efficient Church Secretary effectively communicates with pastors, members, visitors and guests, and staff members with accuracy, clarity, tact and diplomacy. It is one of the core values in the culture of any organization. Healthy communication is a key factor in the success and actualization of the JHDC's Vision of Restoring Hope and Maximizing Potentials (RHAMP).

Let's examine two forms of communication:

1. **Verbal** (oral, spoken): which should be in simple language, be audible, and be specific and in a pleasant tone. Examples are:

a. **Phone Calls**: When receiving calls – first identify the Church name, your office and then yourself. Remember your phone manners must be pleasant so speak in a soft tone, with clarity, be concise, be courteous and get to the point. The use of words like 'hello' - 'please' – 'thank you' - and 'bye' is highly encouraged. Always give the caller your full attention.

b.   **Face to Face**: requires your attention, speak with a soft and friendly tone of voice at all times and smile. It is a means for exchange of thoughts, messages or information.

c.   **Body Language**: be very mindful and watch your body gestures and movements.

2.   **Written** (correspondence by letters, emails, memos, reports): In this age of technology, the Email is the fastest and cheapest way of sending information and correspondence. This medium must be informative and direct, be free of errors and be grammatically correct. It must be written in clear, simple language and short, depending on the subject matter. To make it official, write using letter headed paper or if by email, use brand identity templates which should include a sign-off line. Also, ensure accuracy, proof-read carefully before sending and mailing out.

3. **Public Speaking** is the art of skillful communication in public. These skills can be acquired through intense training and workshops or through Toastmasters Club Meetings for example. At the Toastmasters Club meetings, the group offers professionals and students a supportive environment to improve their skills in communication and leadership. Skills learnt include the ability to participate, to speak or be heard, impromptu speeches; listening and evaluating, etc. Other skills in public speaking include:

Poise – avoid nervousness and stage fright; you must appear calm and confident and avoid distracting behaviors.

Voice – speak with clarity and the right volume.

Life – live life passionately, let it carry-through in how you express your emotions with your voice.

Eye Contact –connect visually with the audience and look at each audience member.

Gestures –You must have an expressive face, move your body and hand in respectful motions.

Speed –speak or talk with appropriate speed, not too slow, not too fast and use pauses for effect and emphasis.

Image and Appearance-

a.   **Clothing:** It is very important to maintain and uphold a professional image and appearance at all times. Remember that your outward appearance is important in communication. At Jesus House DC, our dress code is Business Casual - therefore your dressing, disposition and attitude must reflect and it speaks volumes about the ministry and level of professionalism within it.

b.   **Greetings:** You are encouraged to greet members, visitors and guests as this will set the tone to develop relationship. Depending on your relationship, such greetings must be warm, pleasant, polite and welcoming – remember you are a customer service representative of the Church because every member and guest that you encounter is a potential customer that you will want to retain for growth.

c.   **Premises:** This is where members, visitors and guests congregate or meet for interactions. It must be kept dust-free and clean for comfort at all times – this includes: flowers, chairs, tables, floors, walls, carpets, toilets, kitchen and equipment. As the saying goes – 'cleanliness is next to godliness.' The house of the Lord must be kept clean at all times. This means that janitorial and cleaning services can be considered for regular maintenance.

d.   **Demeanor & Confidentiality:** You have to be conscious that you display a pleasant and positive attitude at work at all times. You must know how to protect the privacy of church members. Whether specifically notified or not, simply make everything private and confidential. Share and relay information only on a need-to-know basis or strictly under Church Leadership directives.

e.   **Networking:** This is very important as you desire to rob minds and expand your interpersonal horizon of relationships with individual members and their businesses. You must have the ability to diversify your network of relationships with members and individuals who have insight and contacts that would promote your job functions and improve your perspectives in life generally. Exercise your power of discernment and follow your instincts to expand your networking experience. God allows you to come across people from all walks of life in church for a reason. Choose to communicate well even in your accent, and speak-up, and let your opinions be heard. Make it a point to participate in professional conferences, trade shows, seminars, workshops and social media groups. In addition to the contacts you could make, don't miss out on the contact information available via flyers, pamphlets and other paraphernalia that goes with these events. Don't forget to circulate and get recognized for your expertise and you will see opportunities to grow.

Volunteering:

To volunteer in the Church is a great way to give of yourself in service to God in His vineyard. It is a way to develop skills and talents that God has deposited in you and to be a blessing in the house of God. In other words - it inspires others to achieve their God-given dreams and potentials. The way to greatness is through service to God, serving one another and serving your community. Doing so would impact many lives for Christ through your activities, actions and contributions. Therefore, at Jesus House, DC, we encourage members to at least commit themselves to volunteering as workers for one year in any ministry or department of their choosing; which their talents, skills and resources can support. The big idea is to mutually impact the various aspects of God's work, as well as the lives of the volunteers. The act of Volunteering enhances and boosts your chances of employment because you're already trained to give your very best in the place of service – something every employer appreciates.

At the Church Office, college and graduate students offer to assist as volunteers in the Accounting, Members Services, and Administration departments etc. Volunteers gain invaluable experiences as they serve. Ultimately, they become transformed into individuals who are useful to humanity, the community, and the corporate market in general. Delegate and assign tasks to volunteers and you will be amazed to see how well they perform. Student volunteers are young with fresh minds and ideas and are ready to challenge the status quo in order to get the best done.

Encourage volunteers to be serious, faithful and committed so they can facilitate moving the service of God and the vision of the church forward.

You can use volunteers effectively for the Lord in the following areas:

- Administration & Accounting

Workplace Ethics & Related Skills

- First Touch Ministries:
    - Protocol
    - Holy Police
    - Ushering
- Children's Ministry (COP & JGEN)
- Caleb Crew Teenage Ministry
- JH Music Ministry
- Branding & Communication
- Visitation & Care Ministry
- Member Services Ministry
- Multimedia (Tech/Video Wall)
- Prayer Ministries
- Xpress (Young Adults & Singles Ministry)
- TLC Evangelism Ministry
- The King's Table Ministry
- Jesus Women Ministries
- Gideon's Men Ministries

- Haggai Business Network (HBN) Ministry
- Daniel Leadership Institute (DLI) Ministry
- Sunday School Ministry
- Hospitality/Welcome Ministry
- One Flesh Marriage Ministry
- Social Media/IT Ministry
- Creative Arts Ministries:
  - Faces – Drama Ministry
  - Expression Dance Team, And many more!!

Leadership:

Leadership is simply defined as influencing people to achieve a goal. It is the ability to bring people together and inspire them to do what they ought to do. Good leaders are not born; they are made and created by circumstances. It is a choice because you choose and accept to be a leader. Therefore, you must put people's interest before your own; and set good examples for others to follow. Integrity and sincerity are also high on the list of the characteristics of a good Leader. Be prepared to be accountable and open to ideas that are not exactly like your own. Be respectful, trust-worthy; and share your opinions without fear of retribution or conflict.

At JHDC all volunteer workers are Leaders. Leadership and empowerment seminars and workshops often conducted and/or attended have prepared many for the important roles they hold in and out of Church. The level of attention and investments in the development of Leadership skills has risen above mere guiding principles to set JHDC apart from other parishes and churches.

JHDC's core guiding principles are:

- Being a *Servant Leader* (to serve with humility and to have a Servant's Heart and Spirit)

- *Ownership* (Taking responsibility and being accountable)

- *Care* (To be intentional about showing that we care)

JHDC strategic anchors for success in Leadership:

- Raising leaders, giving opportunities for new leaders to emerge, and creating succession plans.

- Creativity & Innovation: having a Pioneer's spirit, creating the Wow-Factor and being a Trail-blazer in all we do.

- Excellence: On-time preparation for events and programs is the key. Avoid last minute plans and follow the laid-out plan and processes for flawless execution.

Empowerment:

- Creating opportunities for growth and developing Leaders. Every plan, program or event must leave people empowered to excel in ministry, at work, business, personally in their marriage and family, spiritually and so on.

Love:

- Deliberately creating an atmosphere of love and express same to one another.

Ministers and Heads of Departments must follow these guidelines to bring out the best in volunteer workers:

a. **Mentoring**

Challenges do occur in different areas of life – in career choices, educational choices, marriage relationships, etc. These areas form the arena for mentoring. Mentors and mentees are matched; the mentors guide and share life-impacting perspectives, to help mentees find pathways to fulfilling their lives. The mentoring process may require between 3 to 6 months to a year's commitment between the two parties.

At JHDC, some Ministers mentor members on personal issues. My role is to simply direct members with such requests to the Young Mentoring Program, or Spiritual Faith-Based Counseling or the Marriage Ministry – all of which offer mentoring programs on a one-to-one basis. There are also sessions that pair young professional leaders with individuals or long-standing married couples with newlyweds. The benefits of mentoring cannot be over-emphasized. It boosts membership growth and retention because it adds value to the lives of everyone involved. Most mentees find themselves more engaged as volunteer workers and ultimately happier in their relationships and personal spiritual growth.

b. **Work Life Balance**

Members ask me questions about how I operate the work-life balance given the long hours that I spend at the church Office. Simply put – I answer that "the Lord is my strength". To maintain a balanced work-life, I take 30 minutes break to enjoy lunch, I walk up and down the staircases as a form of exercise or 'hang-out" with coworkers for a while. While a short break is made to refresh the mind, I have also been known to use it sometimes for prayers and or meditation on the Word of God.

I go on annual vacations and take my 2-days off as approved every quarter for total rest or travel. I make time for relaxation by listening to news and documentaries on television, sewing at home, going to see movies, visit friends and attending other social events.

c. **Social Responsibility**

At JHDC, we practice what we preach. The Bibles states in Mark 12:31:

"Thou shalt love thy neighbors as thyself; there is none other commandment greater than these."

We are socially responsible to our street neighbors, businesses and the community around us.

We are socially responsible to our street neighbors, businesses and the community around us. As a staff member, oftentimes I visit business owners around the church to reach-out and to develop relationships or some rapport and to inform them about special events as required by the Montgomery County. I listen to their views and opinions about our church and offer suggestions about how we can improve relationships between us. It was through this neighborly outreach that a certain Auto Shop business offered the Church free use of its parking lots for 3 hours for every Sunday service. We appreciate and love them in return with church souvenir and gifts etc. We also encourage members not to park vehicles or block their property entrances, and not to park on their lawns. We encourage members to be respectful.

We give back through community outreaches. I have participated in outreach events involving cooked food, canned food, winter coat donations etc. to shelters and the less privileged. They are very receptive and welcoming. Some do requests to be prayed for, and ministered to, as they give their lives to Christ.

In a nutshell, you are encouraged to go beyond your comfort zone and scope to do good to your neighbors always. It is so important to develop a good relationship with them all – even if they resent you and your Christian doctrines.

d. **Community Involvement**

I live in Greenbelt, Maryland and I am actively involved in my community as time permits. I volunteer at the Greenbelt community center during the Annual Labor Day Festivals & Parades and I am a member of the Greenbelt Time Bank – a network building the neighborhood and community with our skills, and services based on Time. I am also an appointed and commissioned Notary Public of the State of Maryland; to be part of the dispensation of equal right and justice in every case in which I shall act, under the Commission, and to hold and execute the office justly, honestly and faithfully.

(THE MAYOR OF GREENBELT – EMMETT JORDAN)

"To volunteer in the Church is a great way to give of yourself in service to God in His vineyard." - SMK

CHAPTER 8

Teamwork behind the Scenes

> *"Now I beseech you brethren, by the name of our Lord Jesus Christ, that ye all speak the same thing and that there be no divisions among you; but that ye be perfectly joined together in the same mind and in the same judgment." (1 Corinthians 1:10)*

Teamwork

One of the hallmarks of a good work environment is teamwork. The Church Office cannot operate successfully with only one individual no matter how talented, organized or educated. The ability to work with one another and be accountable to one another cannot be over-emphasized.

At the JHDC Church Office, staff members do a lot behind the scenes to prepare for God-glorifying services, hitch-free events and seamlessly-executed programs. Apart from the Joint Thanksgiving Celebration Service which holds from 10am – 1.00 pm every first Sunday monthly, and Sunday School Class which begins @ 7.30 am., we currently, operate three (3) Sunday services as follows:

- Fresh Anointing Service @ 8.00 am – 9.30 am: Open to all

- Ignite Service is 10.00am – 11.30 am: This is targeted at the ever-growing "Relevant" Young adults & Single Professionals' and more.

- Celebration Service @ 12.00 noon – 2.00 pm: Open to all

I do not perform my work in a vacuum, but I enjoy the total support and cooperation of other staff members. We are a group of dedicated, loyal and hard-working close-knit-family type team. Teamwork is the key – and we have the constant opportunity to bond and facilitate lifelong relationships because we get to know each other better as we work together. We are colleagues who support each other in a friendly work environment and church community. We value each other's opinions and contributions, and show respect to every member of the team, irrespective of what the job titles are. We inspire, encourage and support each other to bring church events into efficient fruition.

We hold Staff Meetings every Monday. These weekly meetings are mandatory and I always look forward to attending and making my presence felt and voice heard. After the meeting's praise and worship session, we pray for the leadership and various ministries while remembering to pray for ourselves and sharing testimonies. We exhort each other focusing on different spiritual topics, and we also read and review leadership, management and spiritual books and resources from which we draw nugget thrown open for discussions.

After work-related deliberations, we come-up with across-the-board actionable solutions for preparedness for the services and events of the week. Tasks are assigned and/or delegated to each staff member, based on the assignments on the table in general and sometimes according to staff member specialties and competencies.

Managing the Church Office With Purpose

(JHDC STAFF MEMBERS)

(WORKSHOP FOR STAFF MEMBERS AT JHDC)

Teamwork behind the Scenes

We hold Staff Treat Days on the second Monday of every month. This is the special time set aside to recognize and celebrate Staff Birthdays with food or snacks including cakes and gift cards. A nominated staff member is appreciated with awards at the annual Appreciation Dinner for Workers and Staff Members. To the glory of God, I am a proud recipient of the following Awards:

1. Staff Appreciation Award in 2011

2. Service Recognition Award in 2012

3. Dedicated Service Award in 2017

Staff members are encouraged to further their education and attend workshops for growth and additional knowledge. We are God's Stewards responsible for the needs of JHDC Ministries and Departments and we strive to meet them to the best of our individual and collective abilities. We are there to offer assistance and our participation to make every program successful and impactful. At times we all chip-in i.e. "all-hands-on-deck" (teamwork) to get things done on time; irrespective of what our primary roles are. You know what they say – Team work makes the Dream work.

The issues discussed and deliberated on at Staff meetings include but are not limited to:

- Reviews of programs and feedback from previous services/events

- Updates to the Calendar of Events

- Identification of the deficiencies/problems that surface during Services/Events to which anyone in the meeting can freely propose potential solutions like:

o Arranging and re-arranging Sanctuary chairs event by event.

o Scheduling Snow removals during inclement weather

o Setting-up & Cleaning-up the Enoch Adeboye Hall pre & post events

o Banquet-Style layout re-arrangement of the Main Sanctuary & Cleaning thereafter

o Engaging landscaping Services around the Church property

o Repair Services - Plumbing, Electrical, A/c & Heating, etc.

Teamwork behind the Scenes

For special projects, the Professional Management Project (PMP) comes into play as selected meetings are done via Conference calls using the Fuze Meeting App. This makes it easy for us to join forces to provide information and assistance when needed in support of special Committees for our Annual Biazo Conference, Annual Prayer Retreats, Annual Prayerthon and Praiseathon, Annual Gideon Men's Conference and the Annual Ultimate Woman Conference, Leadership Retreats/Meetings, Annual Workers/Staff Appreciation Day, etc.

I do share JHDC programs on social media platforms like my Facebook and Twitter. I belong to the WhatsApp groups for Lighthouse Silver Spring 2, Jesus Women Ministries and JHDC Church Staff. Social Media makes it easy to share spiritual information, encourage and celebrate each other's achievements and successes, etc.

I am very humbled, honored and blessed to be surrounded by a very strong, dedicated and capable team of staff members with whom I work to keep the Church of God marching forward. We are happy people who show God's praise and glory in everything we do; and I am really grateful to God for that.

"We are God's Stewards responsible for the needs of JHDC Ministries and Departments and we strive to meet them to the best of our individual and collective abilities." -SMK

CHAPTER 9

Suggested Sample Forms Created

Over the years I have created simple sample forms to make my work better organized and efficient. These forms have made it easy to track requests, services and repairs to be done daily, weekly and monthly. It has improved my performance and made my routine very orderly. I have managed my Outlook calendar with dates from the content of these forms (once they are filled-out); to the end that tracking different projects at varying levels of progress has become easy, because I can consistently follow through.

The advantages:

- It allows you to remember and never miss-out on important dates and upcoming assignments.
- It allows for effective and efficient calendar management.

PASTORAL/SPIRITUAL SUPPORT REQUEST FORM

Date: _____

Name of Member:

_____

Ministry & Department:

_____

I/We would like to formally request the Pastoral & Spiritual Support for my

Family in this area:

- o   Baby Naming Ceremony
- o   Child/Baby Dedication
- o   Service of Songs & Celebration of Life
- o   Wedding Ceremony
- o   Sick/Shut-In/Bereavement
- o   Visitation & Care
- o   House Warming & Dedication
- o   Birthday Thanksgiving
- o   Special Services
- o   Others

Suggested Sample Forms Created

Date of Event: _____

Time of Event: _____

Venue Address:
_____

_____

Email Address:
_____

Telephone Home: _____

Cell: _____

_____   _____
Member Signature   Minister Signature

VEHICLE REQUEST FORM

Person to be transported:
_____

Point of departure:
_____

Destination (full address):
_____

Purpose:
_____

Request made by:
_____

Date:
_____

Description of Vehicle & Tag No.:
_____

Suggested Sample Forms Created

Expected date & time of departure: _____

Odometer Reading: _____

Expected date & time of return: _____

Odometer Reading: _____

Approved by:
_____

Date: _____

Office Manager/Facilities HOD Signature: _____

To be completed by the driver:

Actual time of departure: _____am/pm
Date: _____
Actual time of arrival: _____am/pm
Date: _____

Signature: _____

Date: _____

REGUEST FOR REPAIRS & MAINTENANCE

Date of Request: _____

Repairs/Maintenance Requested By: _____

Reason for Request:
Eg: Men Toilet – 2nd Floor (921 Bldg) Water running

Vendor: _____

Description of Work Performed: _____
Length of Time on Site: Time In: _____ Time Out: _____
Was R&M Satisfactorily Completed? Yes _____ No_____

Suggested Sample Forms Created

If No, What Next? _____

Signed: _____

CHAPTER 10

Relationships with All

> *"As we have therefore opportunity, let us do good unto all men, especially unto them who are of the household of God." (Galatians 6:10)*

> *"Follow peace with all men, and holiness, without which no man shall see the Lord." (Hebrews 12:14)*

It has been an all-round, wonderful experience with JHDC members. Adults, young and old, teenagers and children of all ages have been very supportive and encouraging in every way. Children show respect and good manners in their interactions with me. I am spiritually-fulfilled, my prayers are answered and my life is a testimony to how far the Lord God orders the step of His Beloved.

I never forget that my service is to God first, and then to man, i.e. the various church Ministries, Departments and members as a whole. I do not favor one over another as I deliberately cultivate a cordial and respectful relationship with every member. This humble attitude and disposition makes me more personable and likeable.

The Dos

- You must have an open-door relationship whereby members, visitors and guests can approach you.
- You must be trusted – confidentiality is key (keep their secrets secret).
- You must be believable - for the accuracy of the information you provide etc.
- You must be open jovial without being too sensitive or lacking in sensitivity towards others. Have a good sense of humor and what is and is not appropriate.
- You must be sensitive to their needs or complaints.
- You must make yourself available to assist them and show empathy.
- You must go above and beyond what's required of you, always.

If you do all these and more than God would inspire you to do, you would be well-appreciated and members will remember you in their prayers, praise and thank God for your life and bless you with their gifts and influence etc.

The Don'ts

- You must not intimidate or make people afraid of you in any way.

- You must not embarrass them in any way.

- You must not be too rigid and hard on anyone.

I have had the opportunity to visit members many times at home, in hospitals, or when bereaved or recuperating from sickness or surgery. Take time to do the same. They appreciate me and the church in general for this show of love and kindness.

As JHDC continues to grow, the need for Small Cell and Lighthouse groups cannot be over-emphasized. These smaller groups make it possible to get to know each other more, become knit together in our Walk with Christ the more and of course cause us to be more caring towards one another. I participate actively and have shown how much I care for our members, through Visitor follow-ups, Welfare visitations to those who are shut-in etc. It can be lonely and disheartening to be lost in a crowd, or a large congregation. That's the beauty of these ministry tools and platforms of interaction.

Lighthouse Bible-Study Fellowship (Silver Spring 2)

By default, as a staff member, I am the host of the Lighthouse Bible-Study Fellowship Silver Spring 2. I do organize, setup and prepare to receive members for fellowship. I make sure that light refreshment is served after the meeting. We meet every at different locations within the DC/MD/VA metro area on Wednesdays at 7pm except the first Wednesday of the month that's dedicated to the Holy Communion Service in Church. It is open to every member, their guests and non-members. It is a great, small Bible study group where we hold interactive discussions about the Bible, pray and share testimonies.

My Lighthouse is like a family; because we care and love each other so much. We celebrate special occasions like birthdays, graduations, and other achievements. We organize/participate in other activities such as movies, bowling, concerts, games and more. Every year during the summer season, we invite our friends & family to a community outreach known as "Hello Neighbor". It is an avenue to introduce and discuss the mission of the JHDC Lighthouse Fellowship. "Hello Neighbor" usually takes the form of small picnics, game nights, etc. It's the perfect opportunity for networking in a relaxed atmosphere where light refreshments are served.

(LIGHTHOUSE FELLOWSHIP - SILVER SPRING 2)

The Elders Forum:

I am a member of the Elders Forum ministry which consists of mature adults (male and female), ages 50 years and above. Every member within that particular age bracket is automatically drafted. Our common experiences:

- We are active and retired from different careers.

- We are loving, caring, focused and energetic individuals.

- We are filled with wisdom, knowledge and understanding.

- We are mentors to married couples and the young adults.

- We have experience in diverse and different noble professions.

- We add value to our family and friends.

- We are Role Models, Motivators, Advisers and Encouragers to entire body of Christ.

- We are prayer warriors on behalf of our children, grandchildren and the Church at large.
- We are blessed and happy people.
- We are relevant as we grow old with grace and dignity.

We care for the welfare of each other. We often organize field trips to places of historical and spiritual interest, visit the under-privileged and make donations to good causes and the needy. We meet once a month to spiritually feed on the Word of God and to encourage ourselves in the place of prayer via the conference prayer line and in person.

I thank God for the things He is doing with us, and in us to be blessings to JHDC. My prayer is that our impact will continue to be felt as we build a worthy legacy for posterity.

(THE JHDC ELDERS FORUM – FIELD TRIP OUTINGS)

I am a Jesus Woman:

The Jesus Women Ministries is the women's ministry of Jesus House, DC. Therefore, every female member is a Jesus Woman. Pastor Omo Ghandi-Olaoye is the founder and Pastor-in-Charge of the Jesus Women Ministries, a ministry that addresses pertinent women issues from birth through old age, with a view to positively affecting those areas with the Word of God. She has the calling of God upon her life to preach good news and hope to the poor and the brokenhearted as well as reaching-out to women of all ages with a vision and mission statement to helping them live their full inheritance in Christ Jesus.

The Jesus Women Ministries is managed by volunteers/ordained women-leaders operating in various capacities. They are dependable, reliable, passionate, dedicated, hard-working and God-fearing servants in God's Vineyard. As women-leaders under the leadership of Pastor Omo, it is our responsibility to reach out to other women to bring them in, to serve

To the glory of God, the under-listed ministries have been successfully established and continue to prosper under the Women's Ministry:

1. Joyful Mothers – minister to the spiritual and physical needs of pregnant women.

2. Homebuilders – coach married women for marital success.

3. Proverb 31 – empowers women with financial & investment information.

4. Kingdom Voices - the all-Female choir.

5. Ruth –supports widows.

6. Beulah – ministers to mature single females 30 years and older.

7. Olive Tree Café – an in-house convenience food, drinks and snacks shop.

8. Encounter at Shiloh – ministers to married couples believing in God for children.

9. MOCS – for mothers of children with special needs.

10. MomWise – supports mothers with very young children (infants to 10-year old).

11. And many more

The Ultimate Woman Conference is the women's conference held every year in the first week of June. At these conferences, Guest Speakers are invited to empower and encourage women at different workshops, seminars, breakfast and dinner meetings.

In June 2010, I was recognized for my services to this Ministry and to the Church at large – a certificate award was given to me. Also, in 2017 I won the dress code/Q&A contest at the 'Breakfast at Tiffany' and I was crowned the first-ever Jesus Woman. This award means a lot to me and it really gave me a lot of joy and pride in the work I do. It was an honor and privilege which came with a gift prize. I was so happy and highly elated.

Managing the Church Office With Purpose

EXCERPTS FROM JHDC PAST NEWSLETTER PUBLICATIONS

An Interview with
Sister Mary Kokumo
Church Secretary

What is your official position and what does that entail?
I am the Church Secretary. I am responsible for the daily administrative functioning of the office. I have held this position since September, 1999. The church office keeps records and files for the church and its members. We are essentially the central hub of activity. We relay the needs of the congregants to the relevant departments.

Prior to [JHDC], what did you do?
Before coming to [JHDC] I worked in the diplomatic corp. I worked in the Nigerian Embassy at a point; most recently I was the social secretary to the Ghanaian Ambassador to the United States.

Describe for us, if you will, the challenges associated with working for the church.
Very demanding! Very demanding! The church is large and the members have various issues that require attention. The work requires a tremendous amount of patience, compassion, and empathy. On a daily basis, I receive numerous calls requesting ministerial attention. I have to interview the callers and ascertain the nature of their needs in order to better route the to the appropriate minister or department. I am very pleased with the work that I do and I appreciate the people I work with. The members respect the position.

Compare work with the church to the work that you did previously.
As a social secretary at the embassy, I performed numerous administrative tasks for the ambassador and oversaw the coordination and planning of the social calendar. While my administrative tasks at [JHDC] are not much different from that which I did previously, I must say that it is a blessing to work in the house of God. And I am grateful to Pastor Ghandi for giving me the opportunity.

How did you come about working for [JHDC]?
Well, I first came to know of [JHDC] through Mrs. Abimbola. We met one morning, back when I worked at the embassy. I saw her on the metro and asked her if she was a Christian and if she was African. She invited me to her church and got me in contact with the church office. I called the phone number and Pastor Ghandi picked up the phone. At the time, I wasn't very mobile and I told him I had no means of getting to church. Pastor Ghandi promised that he would pick me up. True to his word, he showed up at my door at 8:30a.m. that Sunday. I have been a member of the church ever since. Pastor Ghandi later called me into his office and offered me the job. It was ordained by God.

Are you happy with the development of the church so far?
We thank God for the increase. I have prospered. The members have prospered. But I know that the Lord hasn't finished with us just yet. The best is yet to come.

Why work for the church?
Well, I considered my own spiritual needs and I decided that I needed to grow. God wanted my here, so here I am. It was quite simply a God ordained step. I am spiritually fulfilled.

DO you have any advice for others who may be considering working for the church?
You should start off as a volunteer first. The church always needs volunteers; plus, it will be you opportunity to find your footing. Sometimes, the job takes on a life of its own.

Relationships with All

ministry PROFILE
something about MARY

There are so many people working behind the scenes to make Jesus House run smoothly. One of such people is Mary Kokumo, popularly known as "Sister Mary." She has been the Church Secretary since September 1998.

Sister Mary works with all the ministries to ensure they are equipped with what they need in order to do their jobs. She is in charge of all the daily administration in the church and also supervises most of the junior staff. She is a very visible face in the church and the friendly voice you hear when you call the main line.

We acknowledge and thank you for the good work you do in Jesus House, DC, and for the love you show us every day and night.

We pray that God continues to strengthen and reward her as she works in His vineyard.

She keeps going even better than the Energizer Bunny!

CHAPTER 11

On a Lighter Note – The Funny Side

"A merry heart maketh a cheerful countenance; but by sorrow of the heart the spirit is broken." (Proverbs 15:13)

I believe God has a sense of humor too. I imagine that He must smile and maybe even laugh at us sometimes because He understands that we are Human. 'Laughter is good medicine' and 'All work and no play makes Jack a dull boy' – as the popular clichés go. Despite the different challenges and spiritual needs around me; it is so amazing to know that there's still humor and jokes that liven my work day. The joys of working at the Church Office abound.

Members' crack me up with jokes which often brings me to tears. These hilarious jokes relieve the stress and pressure of work and my spirit is lifted-up when I laugh. Who says it is not fun to work in the House of the Lord? It is not all spiritual, Christian-ese and holy-holy all the time. We are free to be Humans too and we laugh and joke around.

God has given me a very sweet and shrill voice – so unique that when you hear me speak or sing, it sounds so distinctively melodious. I'm a natural high-soprano. Often times I sing songs in my office to the amazement of my colleagues, who say – "there she goes again", "kingdom voices re-loaded", "Lord, what is my offense?" "Lord, forgive me" they laugh and make fun of me which I enjoy very much.

I am a woman of a particular age – and age comes with experience, wisdom and respect; based on the culture I was raised in. So, members do not call me by my first name. They make-up for this in such a creative and humorous way that I have earned different names and titles including: Sister Mary, Elder Mary, Mommy Office, Mother Mary, Revered Mary, Mommy Mary, The One and Only, Aunty Mae Mae, SisterMary-dot-com, Iya Yard, Pastor Mary, Deaconess Mary, the 411 of JHDC, Mommy Mary and SMK (an acronym of Sister Mary Kokumo) and so forth.

Friendly members and staff mimic the way I speak, and sounds like me in comedies and monologues at different church events and I take it all in stride. Our Drama Production Ministry has mimicked me several times in their drama series; and it always makes the audience laugh and applaud. Jokes bring joy, happiness and laughter which make the work easy and less stressful for me, so I embrace it all.

"I believe God has a sense of humor too. I imagine that He must smile and maybe even laugh at us sometimes because He understands that we are Human." - SMK

CHAPTER 12

Conclusion

> *"Fight the good fight of faith, lay hold on eternal life, whereunto thou art also called, and hast professed a good profession before many witnesses."*
> *(1 Timothy 6:12)*

It has been a great honor, privilege and blessing to be a member, church office staff in such an exalted position in JHDC. I have no regrets whatsoever but I'm filled with gratitude to the Most High God who has given me testimonies galore. God is the most important partner in my journey of life and He has brought me thus far by His grace and mercy. When the history of JHDC is written, I want to be remembered as a pioneer Church Secretary & Office Manager who worked diligently and faithfully. I would also, love members to share how I have impacted their lives to the glory of God.

Working for the church office can be demanding especially for a growing church, but it requires a tremendous amount of good communications, patience, compassion, empathy, care, love, integrity, faithfulness, and much more.

If you are in this line of work or want to be, my advice would be to embrace on your potential gifts and talents; and capitalize on your strength to invent your own way of going above and beyond the call of God on your life. Keep everything simple and natural. Treat everyone in the loving and respectful way you want to be treated.

I have continued to learn through continuous Workforce Development on weekends at the Prince George's Community College at Largo, MD as opportunity arises. Monthly leadership seminars organized at Workers Meetings also enrich my body of knowledge; all contributing to my being able to stand-out, to be who I am today. I have a set goal or purpose to achieve in life. I am focused and not distracted with my circumstances and situations. In addition, my hard work, diligence and devotion to the efficacy of prayers have seen me through.

As my mentor, Pastor Ghandi always challenges and encourages me to do more. Pastor Chinyere Olujide – a successful entrepreneur, experienced and seasoned teacher/speaker, whom I admire and have worked with for several years, also does to the same. Author John Maxwell wrote in one of his books that -

Conclusion

"The secret of your success is determined by your daily agenda – do the right thing and it will set you up for a good start for tomorrow."

In my book, I have detailed a complete representation of my personal approach to work, working relations, interactions with staff members, and or contributions to, and experiences with people I have come across in the church office. Hopefully, it would impact, inspire, and benefit church workers everywhere, Faith-based organizations, ministries, church members and individuals aspiring to fulfil their calling in Church Office Administration and Management positions.

MEMORABLE MOMENTS IN PICTURES

A lot has happened at JHDC. Here are some selected memorable pictures for your viewing pleasure:

(VISIT TO THE WHITE HOUSE EXECUTIVE BUILDING WASHINGTON DC)

Conclusion

(STAFF MEMBERS ON TREAT DAY OUTING TO A MOVIE)

(AT THE ANNUAL BIAZO BALL 2017)

Managing the Church Office With Purpose

(JHDC COMMUNITY OUTREACH EVENT)

REFLECTIONS

From Pastor Omo Ghandi-Olaoye

M ary A. Kokumo is the face of Jesus House, DC. She is our first Touch Personality.

She is the voice that answers the phone and the personality that serves you on the Church's main telephone line anytime a call comes in. Now, you know it is not easy to always be your best 8 hours every work day of the week for 19 years and counting and not having had anyone call to fault your Customer Service Relations in all of those years?

That is our own Sister Mary – Outstanding.

She is a Customer Service Expert extraordinaire.

She is one and a half.

She is the First Touch Office of Jesus House, DC.

She has spoken to more people uncountable number of times, than the total membership of Jesus House, DC. If we were to tabulate the number of personal calls she has made and received in her Office, we would have a stadium full of members. She has spoken to more people over the phone than in person. Her high-pitch Soprano Voice is distinct, peculiar and it precedes her person.

Pastor Bimpe Mfon (Widow of late dear Pastor Eskor Mfon) had spoken too many times with Sister Mary over the phone but has never met her in person though she had visited JHDC severally in the lifetime of her husband and after. On this particular visit, Pastor Bimpe and I were walking into the main building for Sunday Service when she suddenly stopped in her steps and said: Please, where is Sister Mary? I retorted: Sis. Mary? We just walked past her. You didn't see her? Is there something you need? And she said: No. Do you know I don't know her? I have never met her. I was like: Really? These many years?

I immediately turned around with her to go in the direction where we had just walked past Sister Mary. Lo and behold, Sister Mary had sighted me and was herself rushing to catch-up with me for something. Just as we turned around, we came face-to-face with Sister Mary and she immediately went: Pastor, Ekaaro Ma – stretching out her hands to hand some documents over to me. Just as she spoke the greeting, Pastor Bimpe immediately exclaimed: Aaaah ! Sister Mary!! That Voice, the high-pitch Soprano - was unmistakable. Without any introductions it belongs to one and only one person - and would standout anywhere; Anytime!!

Sister Mary apparently had also never met Pastor Bimpe one-on-one. She stood smiling, trying to figure-out and unravel the outburst of laughter and the excitement of the moment. I immediately proceeded to break the ice and make the past-due introductions: Sis. Mary, this is Pastor Bimpe – Pastor Eskor's Wife. This was followed with a handshake, a lot of hugs, acknowledgements and thank-you's (for so many things) from Pastor Bimpe. Sister Mary is in totality, very Nice.

She is mature, very patient, very respectful, friendly, I have never seen her angry or raise her voice at anyone or rub-off on anyone negatively – young or old – in all her years in the Church Office; her rebuke is inoffensive and is always taken very positively. Everything she does, she does with purity and a child-like heart.

Sister Mary is very sincere. I have never known Sister Mary to take offence. She is authentic, dependable, reliable, committed, loyal, tactful, wise, guarded, and humble, has self-control, selfless, ageless, takes initiative, honorable, presentable, however way you want that event or meeting, she will adorn and dress herself to fit the occasion.

Sister Mary will dress the Code. Name it - Formal, Informal, Casual, Dress Casual, and Traditional, Black N Tie/Banquet or Corporate. Sister Mary will represent to the letter. She will turn up right and beautiful and she will conduct herself excellently. You will be proud to go out with and be associated with her.

Sister Mary is beautiful inside out, kind, hardworking, smart, classy, great dresser. She carries herself with dignity and poise. She finds much joy in Service. Sister Mary will always pick up her call. She works great with everyone across board; from the youngest to the oldest - from the junior staff to the CEO. She is very approachable and personable. She does not double-deal. She respects everyone - and, she respects herself.

Sister Mary never went to the Covent. She is not Catholic. Sister Mary is a Senior whose office and duties expose her to different age categories in a 1st World Society. She is pro-active to guard jealously how she is approached in a society where it is not a big deal to call elders by their first names. And so, she stretches out her scepter of respect "SISTER MARY" harmlessly to all, to put all on notice for a Symbiotic Relationship. That is how she personally introduces herself. That is what she signs off on every correspondence that goes out from her desk. That is how she wants to be addressed at the barest minimum. Every other prefix to her name must be an added plus.

Sister Mary is very on top of current affairs and she is very active on Social Media. She listens to the news all day long. Her TV or Radio is always on and at high volume in her Office and at home. And the Channel is always CNN or any other News Channel. Sister Mary is very young at heart. A few years ago, she changed her sign-off from Sister Mary Kokumo to SMK to make it easier for people.

She is known to wear different trendy hairstyles that look so good on her you want to meet her hairdresser. She currently wears an auburn low haircut that is so suitable and trendy for her age. Not only is she very current, trendy, and young at heart, she is also very jolly.

One of the times Sister Mary was with our twins when they were toddlers, they had walked into her room in the morning and innocently played off with an item that looked like a toy. Sister Mary's Wig!!!! Sister Mary cajoled, entreated, lured and reached out to them in diverse ways in vain from within the safety of the room. She kept on calling their names but they continued to walk in the opposite direction away from her. They walked straight into our room with their booty – Sister Mary's Wig! When I saw them, I was wondering what was going on and what they were holding. We retraced our steps back to where they came from and I found Sister Mary in hiding with both her hands on her head as a covering, laughing so heartily saying: Haaah Pastor, awon omo ma ti gbe wig mi lo! (Translation: Pastor, the Children have taken my Wig away). Together, the children and I walked towards her and they handed it over to her. Sister Mary did not want me to see her looking like that. But she was too happy and relieved to have her wig back.

She is a joyful mother and grandmother. Everyone in recognition of her dual roles in Church over the years, have delightfully and joyfully chosen and adopted several other preferred fond pre-fixes for Sister Mary. Aunty Mary, Mom Mary, Mother Mary, Mommy Mary, etc. - all very well deserved.

Wondered where Sister Mary got her Dress sense? She once owned a Boutique in Ibadan, Oyo State, Nigeria. Not only does Sister Mary's high-pitch soprano voice and personality precede her; there's the Ghanaian accent too. She is a full-fledged Nigerian with a Ghanaian accent. Her diet and close relationships reflect it too. Her closest associates are Nigerians and Ghanaians. Once in a while, you will see her dressing laced with Ghanaian touches of Kente or beaded jewelry.

Whenever Sister Mary travels, you will always find Kenke (that Ghanaian Food item that looks like fresh corn on the cob with the leaves) in her luggage. At potluck events, Sister Mary's choice of dish is always Ewa Agonyin – a black-eye beans traditional entrée with stewed fish sauce. This year, she made a donation of this dish in a large quantity during our J-Gen Middle School Church Arm Annual Fundraiser, to be sold and all the proceeds went to the J-Gen Middle School Children.

Sister Mary never travels without bringing back a souvenir gift, food or clothing item from her trip to bless my children and I. She remembers us at Christmas and our Birthdays and never fails to give us gifts.

Sister Mary is the one who has worked the longest with me and closest to me in the Church Office. Sister Mary knows what I want and how I want it; she is always on point and on top. She performs her duties to my Office in different capacities: Executive Assistant, Telephone Calls, Correspondence, Communication, Announcements, Event Scheduling and Reminders, Schedules my Meetings and Reminders, Events Planning and Coordination, Travels, Air Tickets, Logistics, Errands, Drop-Offs, Pick-Ups, Appointments, Orders, Repairs Set up, Break down, Clean up, Guest Services Logistics and Strategy, Sounding Board, Hospitality, Gifts, Airport Runs, Stock-ups, Deliveries, Filings, Record Keeping, Liaising with every other Ministry or Church Office Department, etc.

No duty is too little or too much for Sister Mary. She is never too busy to attend to any need. No one is too little or too old to be honored by Sister Mary. She has knowledge of my Calendar and my Itinerary. She is the one who can reach me anytime and anywhere if my attention is needed on any matter. She will inform me about any matter that requires my information or attention or intervention. She observes Protocol - she ensures that Protocol is observed for me.

Whenever I arrive in the Office, Sister Mary immediately rises up from her Desk to open my Office and let me in, while in addition, relieving me of anything I might be carrying. She has by her actions and in her words, taught the Church Office Staff to do so. If I ever get into the Office before she does, as soon as she settles in, she would either in person or by phone, call to acknowledge, greet and let me know she has arrived. At the end of the day if she has to leave before me, she will also call or come into my Office in person to let me know she is leaving for the day. Sister Mary never ever comes into the Office or leaves the Office without acknowledging me.

When she has to go on vacation, she puts me on notice. And tells me who will be filling in for her in her absence. She ensures that I am comfortable in the Office and all my needs are met in the Office and outside of the Office. Sister Mary knows when I am hungry at work. She will place the order for food, personally serve the food honorably and clear-up after I am done. Sister Mary has remained consistent, unwavering and relentless in her Service. Her standard has remained high and uncompromised.

She is in charge of all my Office Supplies and Maintenance and stocks up accordingly.

She liaises between me and all the other arms of the Church Office Administration. Any work or assignment I am involved in, Sister Mary by extension is involved in.

She is one of those who co-labor with me - on the Parish level and beyond. She is a major anchor for every Jesus Women Event Coordination. Not only does Sister Mary not depart from the event venue until everything is left in absolute order, she is always the last to leave. She is a priceless Support System.

She picks up any telephone call I make to her and acknowledges all my missed calls and returns them promptly – whether she is in the Office, or at Home, or on local trip. Sister Mary is always near.

Thank you.

Whenever I am on an International trip, she is one of the first calls I receive to ensure my safe arrival, comfortability and needs. Especially where I would need to be connected to my family by phone to let them know I arrived safely and to ensure everyone at home is fine. (more so in the days when Cellphones and Sim Cards were not popular and International Calls were expensive). Sister Mary will monitor my arrival especially at the Hotel. A lot of the times, her Phone Calls will coincide with the time the Bell Men are walking me into the Room with my Luggage or as I am just settling into the Room. The Phone rings, the Operator connects, it is Sister Mary's voice on the line saying: Pastor! Welcome. How was your Flight? I hope everything went well? Hold on for the Children. When we are done, she will say: What other calls will you like to make? She then connects me to one urgent work-related call or another – enough to give me peace of mind until my Local Phone Line is activated and I can communicate with her from my end.

She oversees my Pastoral Guests Services and Hospitality. She has over the years come to understand thoroughly how I love to care for our Members and visiting Men and Women of God and all our Guests in General; and she does well to run those assignments for me

She has also learnt to now extend these graces to other aspects in the Church Office Administration

When I was pregnant with our Children, Sister Mary and Olumide Ayoola did the entire Doctors' Visits runs with me. When our Children arrived, Sister Mary was the one entrusted with making the Birth Announcements to all our Friends and Family Members. At times when my husband and I have had to be away on Ministerial Duties, Sister Mary has had to step in sometimes to help care for our children when they were very young.

When I have had to get busy with hours of meetings in Church, Sister Mary ensures that my Children get fed. Besides my husband, Sister Mary is the only other name I have on our Family's Emergency Contact List.

Sister Mary is very accessible - She is reachable. She is diligent, mature, smart, submissive, and teachable, takes disciplinary actions positively and understands implicitly the Call to Ministry. Her world revolves around her Call to Ministry. Sister Mary's temperament is a great delight.

If Sister Mary wants to get you, she knows how to. She would strategically sit and position herself at an angle in front of the Church that you would have no way of escape. She would see you at arrival and confront you with a need that is required of you.

Sister Mary would regularly walk around Church or sit in front of the Church with a Bible Case that erroneously gives her away as an Evangelist. Not quite. This is because, contained in the Bible Case were actually Phone Cards and not Tracts. Sister Mary was a Phone Card Merchant! She would take her position at strategic points in front of the Church as members arrived in Church to enable her identify and collect pending payments from her Phone Cards Debtors and to sell some more. Sister Mary's Goodwill is huge.

Just like everyone else, she is not devoid of some weaknesses. Sister Mary has severally doubly-booked Ministries and Individuals' Events on the Calendar for venues that have caused last minute conflicts. Notwithstanding, in times past when disciplinary actions were taken against Sister Mary by the CEO, members rose up severally en-masse on her behalf to plead that she be reinstated. And it was done. Not only was she forgiven, our Pastor, Spiritual Dad, and CEO promised never to let

Sister Mary off any more on grounds of disciplinary action. That is how much Sister Mary is loved in Church.

If Sister Mary's goodwill in JHDC was to be converted to Dollars, Sister Mary will be a Billionaire. Sister Mary is a woman of very few words. If you are attentive, you will get the gist of her words and her actions and where she is headed. She is observant and understands different personalities and their sincerity of purpose.

Sister Mary is a great Resource/Consultant and Coach on Church Office Staff Management and Ethics. As depicted in the Introductory Paragraph of this Book, everyone that hears the name "Sister Mary" will erroneously think she is a Catholic Reverend Sister. The prefix "Sister Mary" also actually does have a spiritual implication to the fact that God is her Husband, adopted into this Family of the Beloved, and a legitimate member of the Kingdom of God.

I salute, celebrate and honor this Elder Stateswoman of this Body of Christ – Jesus House, DC. Congratulations on this Milestone achievement, an added Feather to your already beautiful Hat, and a Legacy in print that will out-live you.

May all who read your book be lifted and blessed.

REFLECTIONS

From Church Staff and Members

Sister Mary (as she is fondly called) is reliable, humble and wise. She is warm and beautiful within. For a church with a membership of more than 1,300 people that has at least one event every month, she manages administration, secretarial duties, customer service, event planning and coordination, logistics, hospitality and operations. She executes certain duties with love, and always chooses obedience above self. Being of a millennial generation, I am always amazed at how much of herself she is willing to give. Her generosity with service also makes Sister Mary extremely popular in the community.

We tell her that she is most popular because most people who stop by the church first ask for Sister Mary before they ask for anyone else. From the mailmen, to the policemen, to the firefighters, members in the church and in Silver Spring area, everyone knows that in Jesus House DC, Sister Mary is the one that can answer most of your questions. If she doesn't have the answer, she knows when and from whom you can get an answer. People trust her to the point that they would often speak to no-one else in her absence. That shows how loved she is as a member of Jesus House, DC and how dedicated she is at her duties, because her work speaks for itself.

There are leaders who demand your service, and there are those who earn your loyalty. By being an example for us to follow, Sister Mary's life of service makes you willing to do more to please her. She is a woman of grace and virtue, and I am often in awe of her intelligence. When she said she was writing a book, I was not surprised after reading the draft, of how detailed it was because that is the kind of excellence she brings to her job.

I am extremely proud of you, and extremely honored that you chose to have my name in your legacy. I am happy God brought us together, and I pray that this book brings more blessings to you and more glory to the Lord Most High for all that He is still doing through you.

-Vivian Anugo (former JHDC Staff Member)

Community Outreach & Member Care

****

Sister Mary, who I fondly call SMK, is a mother figure in the Church office. She is very approachable, caring to others and truly passionate about her work. She performs her tasks delightfully, without cutting corners. It has been a great privilege to work side by side with her and she is a joy to work with. She takes care of the welfare of the office and the staff which makes her very endearing. She is charming, dresses elegantly, and has a great sense of humor.

SMK loves to laugh and sing, and both are very infectious. She is always punctual and consistent in all that she does both personally and officially, making her very reliable. She loves to learn new things and is trendy about current affairs on the news and in tune with the latest technology. She is not afraid to ask for help or advice where needed to accomplish her tasks.

SMK, I am so delighted about this book, which displays a record of your faithfulness over the years serving in God's vineyard. May this book be a legacy and blessing now and beyond your generation.

-Toks Akinsanmi (former JHDC Staff)
Speaker/Author & Founder of Inspired Scripts

****

As a Co-worker at Jesus House DC, "Sister Mary" as she is popularly called, is a mother in Israel. A loving woman who is kind hearted and always cheerful. She is a hardworking woman who intentionally wants the best for the church - the body of Christ as well as people around her. I find her to be attentive, knowledgeable, trustworthy, caring and compassionate at all times. Her book is a legacy of impeccable experience: the result of great leadership in the ministry."

-Gladys Egbo

JHDC Children's Church – Administrator

****

One Scripture would be the apt summation of my experience with Sister-Mary-dot-com (as I affectionately christened her). And that would be Proverbs 31 verse 29.

"Many daughters [individuals] have done well, but you excel them all." You excel them all in being easily approachable. You excel them all in not using your church position as an excuse to be inhuman and insensitive. You excel them all in love, care, going above and beyond the call of duty. You excelled them all when you personally nursed me back to health for several months in your home after a major surgery which left me barely able to walk. You continue to excel them all, as I have come to experience you as a Believer, to co-worker, and now to member of my own Family (through your knitted heart-connection with my Aunt - your best friend, Mrs. Christiana Adeyeri).

I have watched you pay the high price in your dedication to work and most of all to God, and it's been my pride and joy to see how much God has richly rewarded you. He will continue to reward you forever. Your position in JHDC is NOT for everyone (Romans 12: 5-7). However, EVERYONE CAN BENEFIT from the love and wealth of experience flowing from the pages of this book. So, when you asked me to fulfill the role of the final-cut Editor, I cannot but happily oblige.

Sister-Mary-dot-com, I pray you continue in the spirit of Excellence that Jehovah, your God has endowed you with, and you will surely continue to be preferred above Presidents and Princes, high above all your fellows, from now on and right through to Eternity in Jesus' name, Amen!

Congrats!!! I expect you to write more books in the future. This is just the beginning; but a beautiful beginning it is indeed.

Love Always,
-Ziona Iteoluwakiishi Qing

You can hear her unique voice from a distance as you set eyes on her. Sister Mary, as she is affectionately called, is a real life superwoman, a pivot at Jesus House, DC. She knows all and can do all. In rare occasions when she cannot perform a particular task, she will find someone else to take care of it in a timely fashion. Everybody knows her.

Her office is a one-stop shop throughout the day. She receives and responds to all manner of requests with grace and tact. There is no end to her assigned responsibilities. It is said that no one is indispensable in life but Sister Mary comes really close. I cannot imagine someone else performing this task for so long and with such grace. Her voice and influence is deeply engraved in the JHDC fabric of protocols.

You are greatly loved and admired. Thank you for all you do and your continued sacrifice. I am so glad you are writing this book. It will be a valuable resource to all who read it. May God reward you and continue to watch over you now and always.

-Mercy Luguterah, Ph.D

JHDC Member

References & Resources

1. All scripture quotations are taken from the New King James Version (NKJV)

2. Stephen R. Covey – Author "7 Habits of Highly Effective People"

3. JHDC New Volunteer Worker's Orientation Booklet

4. Notes taken at the conference - New Light Christian Church, Houston, TX.

Connect with
Mary

Facebook

www.facebook.com/sister-marykokumo

Twitter

www.twitter.com/marykokumo

Email

marykokumo@yahoo.com

Made in the USA
Columbia, SC
14 April 2018